WHSmith

Revise

English

KS2: YEAR 6

Age 10–11

Louis Fidge

First published 2007
exclusively for WHSmith by
Hodder Education, an Hachette UK company,
338 Euston Road
London
NW1 3BH

Impression number   10 9 8 7 6 5 4 3
Year   2010

A CIP record for this book is available from the British Library.

Cover illustration by Sally Newton Illustrations

Typeset by Fakenham Photosetting Limited, Fakenham, Norfolk

ISBN 978 0 34094279 6

Printed and bound in Italy.

Contents

Unit 1	Looking for letter patterns	6
Unit 2	Revising verb tenses	7
Unit 3	Word endings – ***ure*** and ***our***	8
Unit 4	Nouns – singular and plural	9
Unit 5	Similes	10
Unit 6	Spelling rules (1)	11
Unit 7	Adverbs (1)	12
Unit 8	Silent letters	13
Unit 9	Clauses (1)	14
Unit 10	Common expressions	15
Unit 11	Pronouns (1)	16
Unit 12	Prefixes	17
Unit 13	Word order in sentences	18
Unit 14	Standard English	19
Unit 15	Connectives (1)	20
Unit 16	Word origins – Latin	21
Unit 17	Prepositions (1)	22
Unit 18	Fun with words (1)	23
Unit 19	Dashes and brackets	24
Unit 20	Alphabetical order	25
Unit 21	Syllables	26
Unit 22	Active and passive verbs	27
Unit 23	Word endings – ***ant*** and ***ent***	28
Unit 24	Nouns – gender	29
Unit 25	Compound adjectives	30

Unit 26   Spelling rules (2) **31**

Unit 27   Adverbs (2) **32**

Unit 28   Tricky spellings **33**

Unit 29   Clauses (2) **34**

Unit 30   Proverbs **35**

Unit 31   Pronouns (2) **36**

Unit 32   Suffixes **37**

Unit 33   Editing sentences **38**

Unit 34   Double negatives **39**

Unit 35   Connectives (2) **40**

Unit 36   Word origins – Greek **41**

Unit 37   Prepositions (2) **42**

Unit 38   Fun with words (2) **43**

Unit 39   Colons and semi-colons **44**

Unit 40   Dictionary work – definitions **45**

             Test 1 . . . . **46**

             Test 2 . . . . **48**

             Test 3 . . . . **50**

             Test 4 . . . . **52**

             Parents' notes **54**

             Answers **57**

The *WHS Revise* series

The *WHS Revise* books enable you to help your child revise and practise important skills taught in school. These skills form part of the National Curriculum and will help your child to improve his or her Maths and English.

Testing in schools

During their time at school all children will undergo a variety of tests. Regular testing is a feature of all schools. It is carried out:

- *informally* – in everyday classroom activities your child's teacher is continually assessing and observing your child's performance in a general way
- *formally* – more regular formal testing helps the teacher check your child's progress in specific areas.

Testing is important because it:

- provides evidence of your child's achievement and progress
- helps the teacher decide which skills to focus on with your child
- helps compare how different children are progressing.

The importance of revision

Regular revision is important to ensure your child remembers and practises skills he or she has been taught. These books will help your child revise and test his or her knowledge of some of the things he or she will be expected to know. They will help you prepare your child to be in a better position to face tests in school with confidence.

How to use this book

Units

This book is divided into forty units, each focusing on one key skill. Each unit begins with a **Remember** section, which introduces and revises essential information about the particular skill covered. If possible, read and discuss this with your child to ensure he or she understands it.

This is followed by a **Have a go** section, which contains a number of activities to help your child revise the topic thoroughly and use the skill effectively. Usually, your child should be able to do these activities fairly independently.

Revision tests

There are four revision tests in the book (pages 46–53). These test the skills covered in the preceding units and assess your child's progress and understanding. They can be marked by you or by your child. Your child should fill in his or her test score for each test in the space provided. This will provide a visual record of your child's progress and an instant sense of confidence and achievement.

Parents' notes

The parents' notes (on pages 54–56) provide you with brief information on each skill and explain why it is important.

Answers

Answers to the unit questions and tests may be found on pages 57–64.

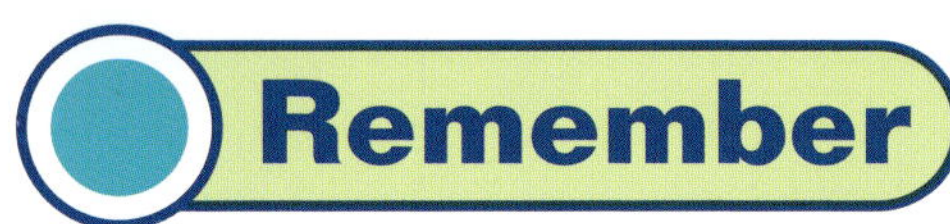

It is helpful to look for **common letter patterns** in groups of words.
This can help us to remember their spellings.

dol**ph**in　　　　　　　　**ph**antom

Sort the words in the box into sets according to their common letter patterns.
There will be three words in each set. One set has been done for you.

boredom	examination	choir	pause	education	learn
conversation	freedom	hedge	character	saucer	ledge
search	wedge	author	early	kingdom	chemist

'dom' words	'______' words	'______' words
boredom		
freedom		
kingdom		

'______' words	'______' words	'______' words

Unit 2: Revising verb tenses

Remember

The **tense** of the verb tells us when an action took place.

Yesterday I **went** to the park.

Now I **am going** to the shop.

Tomorrow I **will go** on holiday.

This happened in the **past**. The verb is in the **past tense**.

This is happening **now**. The verb is in the **present tense**.

This will happen in the **future**. The verb is in the **future tense**.

Have a go

1 Complete the table.

verb	present tense	past tense	future tense
dig	I am digging	I dug	I will dig
break	I am breaking		
driving	I am driving		
fly			
push			
sit			
write			
sleep			

2 Change the verbs in these sentences from the past tense to the future tense.

   a Tom went to the shed.   **Tom will go to the shed.**

   b He put on his boots.   _______________________________

   c Tom picked up a fork.   _______________________________

   d He dug the garden.   _______________________________

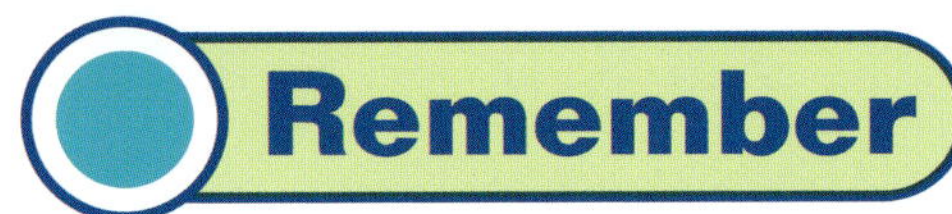

Unit 3: Word endings – *ure* and *our*

Remember

Many words **end** in the same way.
Learn the spelling of some **common word endings**.
Both of these common word endings often **sound the same**.

treas**ure**

glam**our**

Have a go

1   Make some words. Read the words you make.

a   **ure**

nat**ure**   fail___   fig___   treas___   meas___

nature   _________   _________   _________   _________

b   **our**

col___   arm___   fav___   hon___   harb___

_________   _________   _________   _________   _________

2   Find five **ure** and five **our** words in the puzzle.

Write them here.

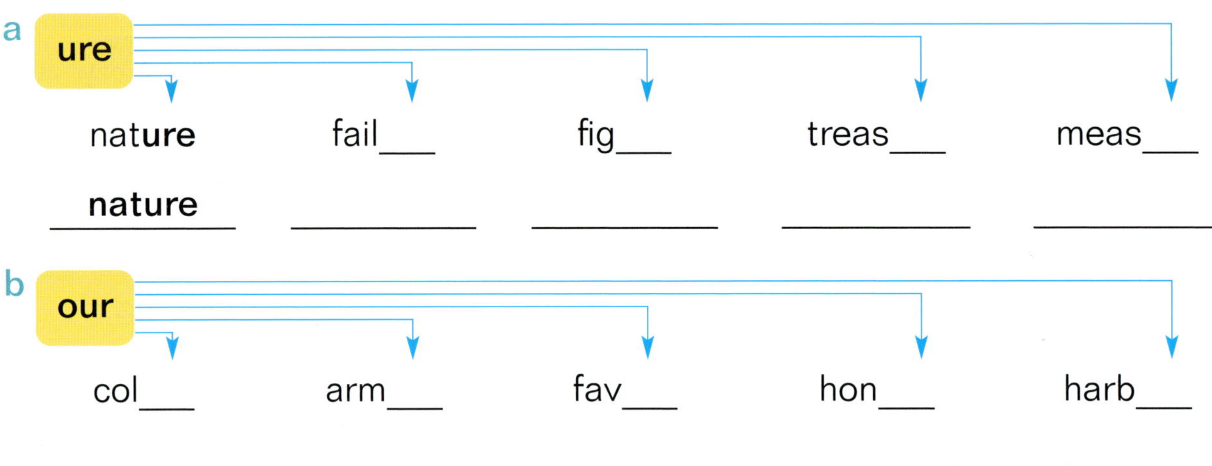

fixture _________________________

____

____

____

____

____

____

____

____

 Unit 4: Nouns – singular and plural

 **Remember**

A **noun** is a **naming** word. Nouns may be **singular** (when there is only **one**) or **plural** (when there is **more than one**).

one potato

a sack of potatoes

 **Have a go**

Follow the rules. Fill in the missing plurals.
Think of another word to prove each rule.

rules for changing singular nouns to plural	singular	plural
a We just add **s** to most nouns.	cat ________	cats ________ ________
b When a noun ends with a vowel + **y**, we just add **s**.	tray ________	________ ________
c When a noun ends with a consonant + **y**, we change the **y** to **i** and add **es**.	lady ________	________ ________
d When a noun ends with **s**, **x**, **ch** or **sh**, we add **es**.	bush ________	________ ________
e When a noun ends with **f** or **fe**, we change the **f** or **fe** to **v** and add **es**.	knife ________	________ ________
f When a noun ends with a consonant + **o**, we usually add **es**.	tomato ________	________ ________
g When a noun ends with a vowel + **o**, we usually just add **s**.	radio ________	________ ________
h Some nouns stay the same in both the singular and the plural.	sheep ________	________ ________

Unit 5: Similes

Remember

A **simile** compares **two** things. Similes contain **adjectives**.

as quiet as a mouse

Have a go

1 Use the adjectives in the box to complete these common similes.

flat	sharp	blind	keen	wise
hot	gentle	fit	slippery	thin

a as _______ as a bat

b as _______ as a dove

c as _______ as a razor

d as _______ as fire

e as _______ as an eel

f as _______ as a rake

g as _______ as a pancake

h as _______ as an owl

i as _______ as a fiddle

j as _______ as mustard

2 Think of a suitable adjective to complete each simile.

a as _______ as a mouse

b as _______ as a lamb

c as _______ as a rock

d as _______ as the sea

e as _______ as a thief

f as _______ as a knight

g as _______ as dust

h as _______ as silk

i as _______ as lightning

j as _______ as rain

k as _______ as a feather

l as _______ as cotton wool

Unit 6: Spelling rules (1)

Remember

Some **spelling rules** are helpful to remember.
One rule to learn is:
When we add **y** to a word ending in **e**, we drop the **e** before adding the **y**.

noise + y = noisy

Have a go

1 Follow the rule and write the answers to these word sums.

  a ice + y = ______
  b lace + y = ______
  c stone + y = ______

  d noise + y = ______
  e breeze + y = ______
  f edge + y = ______

  g smoke + y = ______
  h wire + y = ______
  i juice + y = ______

  j laze + y = ______
  k shade + y = ______
  l haze + y = ______

2 Write the words you made in question 1 in alphabetical order:

____

____

____

____

____

____

____

____

____

____

3 Take the **y** off the adjectives.
Write the nouns you are left with.

adjectives	nouns
smoky	smoke
juicy	
hazy	
icy	
stony	
lazy	
shady	
wiry	
breezy	
edgy	
lacy	
noisy	

Unit 7: Adverbs (1)

Remember

An **adverb** tells us more about a **verb**.

The wind howled **loudly**.

Have a go

1 Underline all the verbs. Circle all the adverbs.

a The woman laughed happily.

b The cat sat quietly on the mat.

c In the exam, the boy wrote quickly.

d The knight fought bravely.

e The people in the queue waited patiently.

f Sam wearily plodded home.

g Suddenly the door opened.

h The footballer skilfully dribbled past his opponent.

2 Match up each adverb with the verb it best describes.

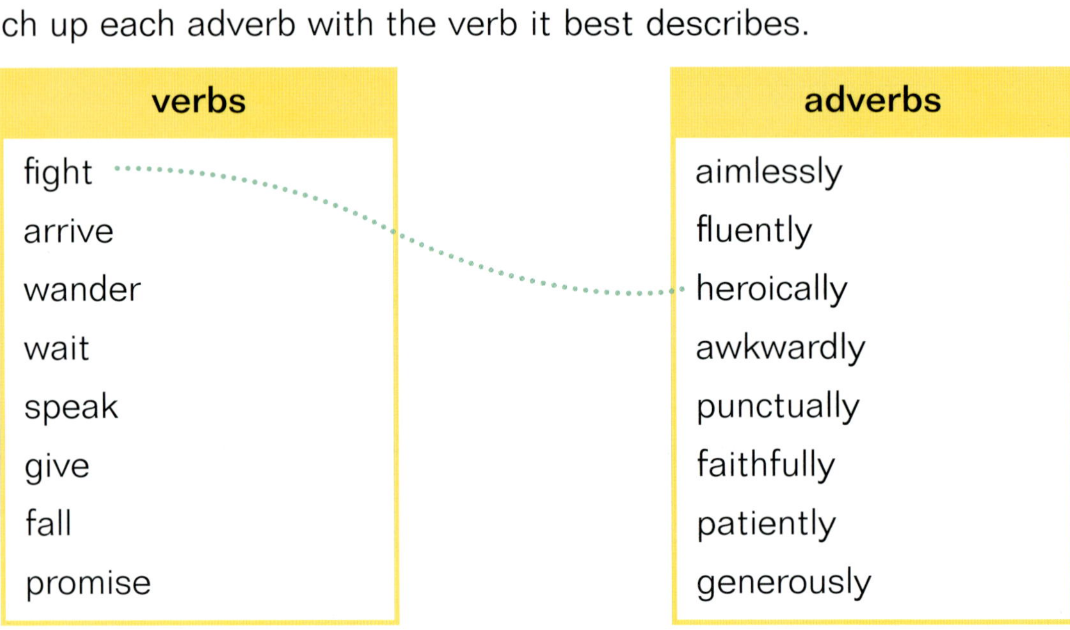

verbs	adverbs
fight	aimlessly
arrive	fluently
wander	heroically
wait	awkwardly
speak	punctually
give	faithfully
fall	patiently
promise	generously

Unit 8: Silent letters

Remember

Some words contain **silent letters**.
We cannot hear these letters when we say the words.

knot   lam**b**

Have a go

1 Fill in the missing silent **g**, **k** or **w** in each word.
Use a dictionary if necessary.

a   **k**now

   know

b   ___nu

   ____

c   ___reck

   ____

d   ___narled

   ____

e   ___not

   ____

f   ___rite

   ____

g   ___neel

   ____

h   ___rap

   ____

i   ___riggle

   ____

j   ___nat

   ____

k   ___nuckle

   ____

l   ___rinkle

   ____

2 Match these words up with their meanings.

gnu	to get down on your knees
know	a large African antelope
wreck	to put words on paper for people to read
gnarled	to understand and remember something
knot	to damage something so it cannot be used again
write	one of the places where your fingers bend
kneel	twisted like the trunk of an old tree
wrap	the twisted part where something has been tied together
wriggle	to twist and turn the body like a worm
gnat	a small crease in the skin
knuckle	a small fly that bites
wrinkle	to put cloth or paper round something

Unit 9: Clauses (1)

Remember

A **clause** is a **group of words** which may be used as a **whole sentence**, or as **part of a sentence**. A clause must contain a **verb** and usually a **subject**.

The spacecraft landed on the moon.

↑   ↑

subject   verb

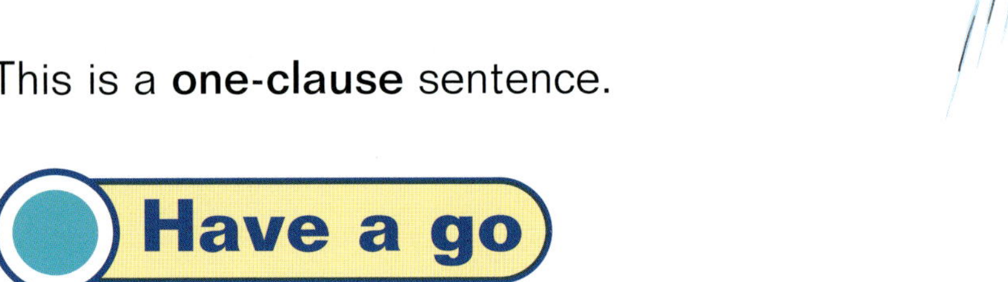

This is a **one-clause** sentence.

Have a go

1 Underline the subject and circle the verb in each one-clause sentence.

   a The monkey pulled a funny face.
   b The girl walked over the bridge.
   c The children entered the museum.
   d Toby scored the winning goal.
   e Sharks swim in the sea.
   f The dinosaur roared loudly.
   g We found a crab in the rockpool.
   h Pandas eat bamboo shoots.

2 Underline the verbs in the sentences.
Say if each sentence consists of one or two clauses.

   a I like Saturdays because we go to town. (**2**)
   b The fox hunted for food in the forest. (__)
   c The sun shone and the wind blew. (__)
   d I ate the curry and rice hungrily. (__)
   e The story started in an exciting manner. (__)
   f Lions show their teeth when they roar. (__)
   g I bought a comic when the shop opened. (__)
   h The old lady drove very fast. (__)

Unit 10: Common expressions

Remember

In **different areas** of the country people have **different ways of saying the same things**. This use of words or grammar is called a **dialect**. Many people from the East End of London, often called Cockneys, have developed a dialect called **Cockney rhyming slang**.

In Cockney rhyming slang 'loaf of bread' really means 'head', as in 'Use your loaf'.

Have a go

Match up each Cockney rhyming slang expression with what it means.

bacon and eggs	house
bees and honey	phone
boat race	legs
cat and mouse	cupboard
daisy roots	car
dog and bone	money
frog and toad	boots
jam jar	clock
mince pies	face
Mother Hubbard	feet
north and south	road
plates of meat	mouth
dickory dock	eyes

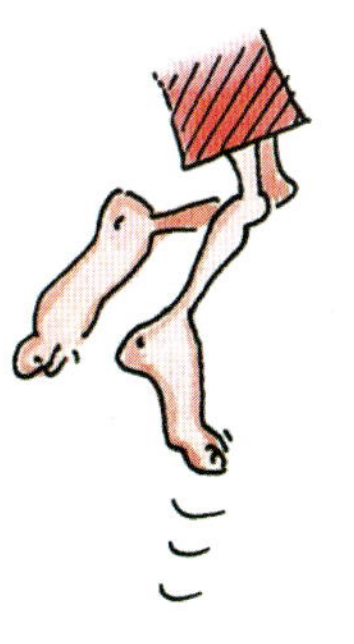

Unit 11: Pronouns (1)

Remember

A **pronoun** is a word that **takes the place of a noun**.

Tom got muddy when **he** (Tom) fell over.

This is my bag not **yours** (your bag)!

Personal pronouns are used in place of **people** or **things**.

Possessive pronouns show **who** or **what** owns them.

Have a go

1 Work out who or what each underlined personal pronoun stands for.

  a When James picked up the pencil <u>he</u> (_______) broke <u>it</u> (___________).

  b Sophie has a TV in her bedroom. <u>She</u> (______) is always watching <u>it</u> (_____).

  c "<u>I</u> (_________) love music," Mr Jones said.

  d "Come with <u>us</u> (____________)," Amy and Emily said.

  e The man wanted the trousers but <u>they</u> (____________) were too dear for <u>him</u> (______).

  f The cows mooed at the girl when <u>they</u> (_________) saw <u>her</u> (_________) coming.

  g The alien stopped when <u>it</u> (____________) heard the noise.

  h "Apples are good for <u>you</u> (_________)," Mrs Butt told Jenny.

2 Choose the best possessive pronoun to complete each sentence.

  a You can't have that ball. It's __________ (my/mine).

  b The girl was not sure whether the bag was __________ (her/hers).

  c The boy found a pen. It was __________ (he/his).

  d The teacher looked at some pictures. "Do you like __________ (our/ours)?" Luke and Alex asked.

  e "Are these __________ (your/yours)?" the teacher asked Amy, and showed her some trainers.

  f When I looked at Mr and Mrs Smith's car, I liked __________ (their/theirs) better than __________ (mine/my).

Remember

A **prefix** is a group of letters that goes **in front** of a word. Prefixes change the **meanings** of words.

✓ approve

✗ **dis**approve

Have a go

1 Choose the best prefix to make a sensible word.

a
after	anti

______clockwise

b
be	bi

______friend

c
centi	circum

______metre

d
de	di

______fend

e
em	ex

______change

f
il	im

______patient

g
mid	mis

______day

h
multi	mono

______purpose

i
under	over

______cast

j
post	pre

______arrange

k
super	sub

______marine

l
trans	tri

______port

2 Take the prefix off each word. Write the word you are left with.

a	amphitheatre	theatre_______	**b**	disability ____________
c	encircle	____________	**d**	exchange ____________
e	foretell	____________	**f**	hemisphere ____________
g	hyperactive	____________	**h**	import ____________
i	kilometre	____________	**j**	midnight ____________
k	misjudge	____________	**l**	nonsense ____________
m	overbalance	____________	**n**	postdate ____________
o	surmount	____________	**p**	uphill ____________

Remember

Sometimes we can **change the order of words** within a sentence **without changing the meaning** of the sentence.

The cat crept silently through the grass.
Silently the cat crept through the grass.

1 Rewrite each sentence. Begin the sentence with the underlined words.

a "Come quickly!" <u>the children shouted</u>.

____

b "I'm going out," <u>Tom called</u>.

____

c "The grass needs cutting," <u>the man said</u>.

____

d "Can I come with you?" <u>Sam asked</u>.

____

e "I want a drink," <u>Harry moaned</u>.

____

f "Have you seen my bag?" <u>Mary asked</u>.

____

2 Underline the adverb in each sentence.
Rewrite each sentence and begin it with the adverb.

a The explorer faced the lion <u>bravely</u>.

____

b Anna wrote in her book neatly.

____

c The children whispered together quietly.

____

d I read the question slowly.

____

e The car appeared suddenly.

____

f I slammed the door noisily.

____

Unit 14: Standard English

Standard English is thought of as the 'correct' form of written English used in schools, business and government.
Non-standard English is often used in everyday speech.

Me and Tom played footie.

Tom and I played football.

This is in **non-standard** English.

This is in **standard** English.

1 Tick the sentence in each pair which is written in standard English.

a	Me and Sam watched telly.	Sam and I watched television.	
b	Who has got my pencil?	Who's got me pencil?	
c	They are coming soon.	They comin' soon.	
d	I didn't see nuffin'.	I did not see anything.	
e	I ain't going nowhere.	I am not going anywhere.	
f	What are you staring at?	What you staring at?	
g	We was just going out.	We were just going out.	
h	Here are the sweets that I bought.	Here's the sweets what I bought.	

2 Match each pair of sentences.

non-standard English	standard English
Sam ain't here.	Tom and I went home.
We done it yesterday.	I want a big cake.
Me and Tom went home.	Sam is not here.
Me socks was in me bag.	I'm going to play outside.
I wanna big cake.	We did it yesterday.
What yer want?	That's really naughty.
I'm gonna play outside.	My socks were in my bag.
That's real naughty.	What do you want?

Unit 15: Connectives (1)

Remember

Connectives are words or phrases that can **join** together **ideas** or **sentences**. A connective may be a **single** word or **more than one** word.

Jack was out of breath, **but nevertheless** he still kept running.

Have a go

1 Underline the connectives in these sentences.

a The cat was happy so it purred loudly.

b Sarah can come for the weekend if she helps with the jobs.

c I don't want to stay because it's too crowded.

d The gymnast won a gold medal although she was only twelve.

e The car pulled away before the light turned green.

f I finished first therefore I deserve the prize.

g I ate an apple while I watched TV.

h I am always lucky whereas John never wins anything.

2 Choose the best connective to join the two clauses in each sentence.

a I went to bed _______ I could get some sleep. (so that/as)

b I visit my uncle _______ I have time. (in case/whenever)

c I try to do my homework _______ I watch TV. (although/before)

d The cat chased the bird _______ it flew down. (since/when)

e I could go to the park _______ the cinema. (or/as)

f I didn't stop shouting _______ I was told to. (until/during)

g We will miss the bus _______ we will be late. (if/so)

h We escaped from the car _______ it crashed. (where/when)

Remember

The English language has been influenced by **many other languages**.
Understanding the **origins** of words sometimes help us to spell them.
Many of our words have their origins in the **Latin** language of the Romans.

In Latin **audio** means **I hear**.

From the word **audio** we get the word **audience**.

Have a go

1 Match up each Latin word with an English word which comes from it.

Latin words	English words
signum (meaning a sign)	spectator
scribere (meaning to write)	video
spectare (meaning to look)	signature
videre (meaning to see)	flexible
flectere (meaning to bend)	scribble

2 Sort these words into sets according to their Latin origins.

audience	prime	aqualung	circular	primary
audible	circuit	describe	primate	aquaplane
scribble	auditorium	aquarium	manuscript	circumference

aqua meaning water	audio meaning I hear	scribo meaning I write	circa meaning around	primus meaning first
aqualung				

Unit 17: Prepositions (1)

Remember

A **preposition** often tells us about the **position** of something or someone in relation to someone or something else.

Prepositions are usually placed **in front of nouns** or **pronouns** in sentences.

The snail is **on** the wall.

Have a go

1 Underline the preposition in each sentence.

a There were four eggs in the nest.

b The child stared insolently at the lady.

c The man rowed the boat across the river.

d The garage is behind the house.

e The children strolled through the woods.

f The horse jumped over the fence.

g The beetle was under the rock.

h Lots of houses were destroyed during the hurricane.

2 Choose the best preposition to complete each sentence.

a The cake was shared _________ (before/between) the two children.

b The burglar crept _________ (across/past) the police officer.

c The swimmer dived _________ (in/into) the pool.

d The tree stood _________ (above/behind) the house.

e The traffic jam stretched _________ (along/among) the road.

f A stone was thrown _________ (by/through) the window.

g The man leant his ladder _________ (about/against) the wall.

h The athlete ran _________ (around/aboard) the track.

Unit 18: Fun with words (1)

Remember

Playing with words can help us learn more about **spelling**.

If we take **art** out of **starting** we are left with **sting**!

Have a go

Take the small word out of the longer word and see what you are left with.

longer word	word to take out	shorter word left
basket	ask	**bet**
capable	cap	
surface	surf	
blade	lad	
bargain	gain	
paint	in	
mallet	all	
balanced	lance	
threading	read	
before	for	
garages	rage	
father	the	
snowing	now	
money	one	
feared	ear	
slowly	owl	
wanted	ant	
colossal	loss	
puppies	pup	

Remember

Punctuation marks help the reader **make sense** of a text.

> A **dash** holds words apart. It is stronger than a comma, but not as strong as a full stop.

> **Brackets** enclose information to separate it from the rest of the sentence.

I visited my favourite city – London.

London (the capital of England) is a large city.

Have a go

1 Choose the most sensible ending to follow each dash.

I bought some fruit –	sausage and chips.
My sister loves cabbage –	'The Haunted House'.
It was my favourite meal –	a bunch of bananas.
At school Amy won a cup –	Liverpool.
I saw a scary film on TV –	I hate it!
Hand in your work on Monday –	one was very scruffy.
I saw my favourite team –	at the latest!
One man was dressed smartly –	Best Sportsgirl Cup.

2 Choose the best 'filling' for each pair of brackets, and write in the letter.

> A (a football team)   D (Mount Kilimanjaro) G (deciduous trees)
> B (a famous writer)   E (London)   H (a bird of prey)
> C (five interlinking rings) F (December 31st)

a Some trees (__________) lose their leaves in autumn.

b The hawk (__________) has a hooked beak.

c Newcastle United (__________) wear white and black striped shirts.

d The capital of England (__________) is full of traffic.

e The Olympic symbol (__________) is well-known.

f The highest mountain in Africa (__________) always has snow at the top.

g New Year's Eve (__________) is known as Hogmanay in Scotland.

h William Shakespeare (__________) was born in Stratford-upon-Avon.

Unit 20: Alphabetical order

Remember

Dictionaries are organised in **alphabetical order**.

These words are arranged in alphabetical order.

post**a**ge   the money paid for a stamp

post**c**ard   a card on which a message may be sent by post

post**m**ark   the mark stamped on a letter by the post office

Have a go

Write each set of words in alphabetical order.

a
behalf
behold
behave
behind

_____________ _____________ _____________ _____________

b
handcuff
handwriting
handbag
handiwork

_____________ _____________ _____________ _____________

c
subside
subsequent
substitute
subscribe

_____________ _____________ _____________ _____________

d
goldfish
goldsmith
golden
goldmine

_____________ _____________ _____________ _____________

e
transfer
transact
translate
transmit

_____________ _____________ _____________ _____________

f
collapse
collect
collaborate
college

_____________ _____________ _____________ _____________

Unit 21: Syllables

Remember

Words may be broken down into **smaller parts**, called **syllables**, when we say them slowly. Every syllable must contain at least **one** vowel.

fin – ish – ing
(3 syllables)

Have a go

1 Do the syllable sums and write the words you make.

a con + duct + or = ____________

b pun + ish + ment = ____________

c in + tro + duce = ____________

d in + sult + ing = ____________

e care + ful + ly = ____________

f trans + port + ed = ____________

g dis + ap + pear = ____________

h re + flec + tion = ____________

i sig + nat + ure = ____________

j lib + er + ty = ____________

2 Think of a suitable second syllable for each word. Write the whole word you make.

a ac + **ro** + bat = **acrobat**

b lem + _____ + ade = __________

c Sep + _____ + ber = __________

d pro + _____ + sal = __________

e u + _____ + form = __________

f es + _____ + lish = __________

g hos + _____ + al = __________

h at + _____ + tion = __________

i dis + _____ + ver = __________

j help + _____ + ness = __________

k ten + _____ + ly = __________

l ex + _____ + tion = __________

Unit 22: Active and passive verbs

Remember

A verb is **active** when the **subject** of the sentence **performs the action**.

A verb is **passive** when the **subject** of the sentence has the **action done to it**.

The girl **ate** the cake.   The cake **was eaten** by the girl.

Have a go

1 Match up the active and passive form of each sentence.

active form	passive form
The boy painted the picture. The pirate waved a sword. The woman carried a bag. Sam read a book. The man planted some seeds. The squirrel hid the nuts.	A bag was carried by the woman. Some seeds were planted by the man. The nuts were hidden by the squirrel. A book was read by Sam. A sword was waved by the pirate. The picture was painted by the boy.

2 Rewrite each sentence. Change the verb from the passive to the active.

a The bridge was crossed over by the car.

The car crossed over the bridge.

b Many books were written by Roald Dahl.

____

c The house was broken into by the burglar.

____

d The palace was guarded by soldiers.

____

e The can of beans was opened by Mr Griggs.

____

Unit 23: Word endings – *ant* and *ent*

Remember

Many words **end** in the same way.
These two common word endings often **sound the same**.

arrog**ant**

obedi**ent**

Have a go

1 Make these words.

arrog		**arrogant**
abund	**ant**	__________
extravag		__________
ignor		__________
fragr		__________

obedi		__________
intellig	**ent**	__________
magnific		__________
viol		__________
evid		__________

2 Match the words you make to their meanings. Use a dictionary if necessary.

a ____________ = willing to do as told   b ____________ = easily seen

c ____________ = spending a lot of money   d ____________ = very grand

e ____________ = sweet-smelling   f ____________ = plentiful

g ____________ = not knowing much   h ____________ = haughty

i ____________ = very strong and rough   j ____________ = clever

3 Choose **ant** or **ent** to complete each word.

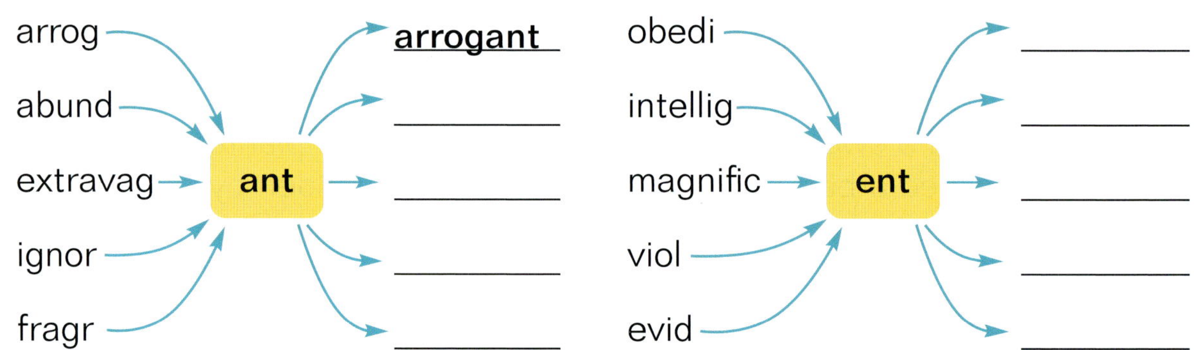

a assist____   b mut___   c abs___   d import___   e eleg___

f sil___   g differ___   h dist___   i defi___   j conveni___

Unit 24: Nouns – gender

Remember

Nouns (naming words) may be divided according to their **gender**.

a boy

a girl

a teacher

a book

Nouns which refer to **males** are **masculine** nouns.

Nouns which refer to **females** are **feminine** nouns.

Nouns which may refer to **either** a male **or** a female have a **common** gender.

This is a **neuter** noun. Neuter means **without gender**.

Have a go

1. Write the nouns correctly in the table.

niece	husband	fork	pupil	uncle	bull
guest	nun	bride	camera	traveller	hotel
doctor	friend	lioness	prince	car	patient

masculine	feminine	common	neuter

2. Write the nouns that are being described.
   Say if they are masculine (m), feminine (f), common (c) or neuter (n).

description	answer	gender
a woman in charge of a school		
a child whose parents are dead		
a son of a king		
the place where prisoners are kept		
the opposite of a daughter		
someone who writes books		
a utensil you use to cut food		
the daughter of a queen		

Unit 25: Compound adjectives

Remember

An **adjective** is a **describing** word. **Compound** adjectives are made up of **two** words. When they are used in front of a noun they are usually joined together with a **hyphen**.

I love **fresh-smelling** bread.

Have a go

1 Put hyphens in these compound adjectives.

a angry looking	b ice cold	c well known
d clean shaven	e long haired	f three wheeled
g pet loving	h light headed	i hard working
j football mad	k shabby looking	l light fingered

2 Use the compound adjectives you made to complete these sentences:

a The ________________ pop singer appeared on TV.

b The ________________ fan went to every single match.

c I felt sorry for the ________________ beggar.

d The ________________ man didn't stop work until nearly midnight.

e The ________________ boy badly needed a haircut.

f Someone who is ________________ steals a lot.

g I was so hot that the ________________ drink tasted wonderful.

h A tricycle is a ________________ vehicle.

i The ________________ motorist hooted his horn and shook his fist.

j The ________________ child had six mice, two dogs, a cat and a parrot.

k Someone without a beard is ________________.

l The thin atmosphere made me feel ________________.

Unit 26: Spelling rules (2)

Remember

Some **spelling rules** are helpful to remember.
One common rule is:
Always put **i** (when it makes the sound **ee**) before **e** except after **c**.

chief   ceiling

Have a go

1 Make some **ie** words.

	ie		

th<u>ie</u>f   f____ld   sh____ld   p____ce   n____ce

__thief__   ________   ________   ________   ________

br____f   f____rce   p____rce   ach____ve   bel____ve

________   ________   ________   ________   ________

2 Follow the rule above. Complete these words with **ie** or **ei**.

a shr___k   b rec___ve   c pr___st   d c___ling   e misch___f

f p___ce   g dec___ve   h sh___ld   i rel___f   j conc___t

k y___ld   l bel___ve   m rec___pt   n gr___f   o perc___ve

3 Write the words you made in question 2 in the table below.

ie words	ei words

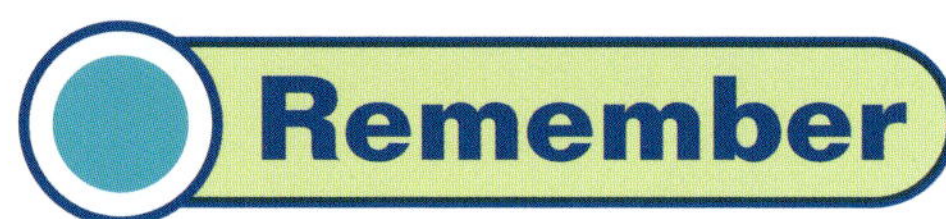

Remember

An **adverb** tells us more about a **verb**. There are different **types of adverb**.

A girl was **quietly** reading her book.

A few minutes **later** she stopped.

She went **outside**.

An adverb of **manner** answers the question 'How?'

An adverb of **time** answers the question 'When?'

An adverb of **place** answers the question 'Where?'

Have a go

1 Underline the adverb in each sentence. Say if it is an adverb of manner (M), time (T) or place (P).

a Mrs Smith answered sharply. (__)

b Our visitors arrived yesterday. (__)

c Will you be there? (__)

d We seldom see each other. (__)

e I turned the box around. (__)

f I slept very badly. (__)

g Tomorrow I am going swimming. (__)

h We looked everywhere for the key. (__)

2 Make up some sentences of your own. Include the following adverbs in them:

wisely (M)	soon (T)	here (P)	bravely (M)
seldom (T)	nowhere (P)	furiously (M)	nowadays (T)

____

____

____

Remember

When adding a suffix beginning with **a** or **o** after a 'soft' **c** or **g**, always retain the **silent e** to keep the **c** or **g** 'soft'.

notice + able = notic**e**able

courage + ous = courag**e**ous

Have a go

1 Rewrite each of these words correctly.

a tracable **traceable**

b noticable _______________

c changable _______________

d managable _______________

e couragous _______________

f advantagous _______________

g peacable _______________

h servicable _______________

i chargable _______________

j enforcable _______________

k replacable _______________

l outragous _______________

2 Write the words correctly in the table below.

able words	**ous** words

Unit 29: Clauses (2)

Remember

A **clause** is a **group of words** which may be used as a **whole sentence**, or as **part of a sentence**. Each clause must contain a **verb**.

I <u>picked</u> some flowers.
(verb)

(clause 1)
I <u>picked</u> some flowers
(verb)

(clause 2)
which <u>grew</u> in my garden.
(verb)

A **simple sentence** is made up of just **one clause**.

A **complex sentence** is made of **more than one clause**.

Have a go

1 Match up pairs of clauses to make sensible complex sentences.

a	I cleaned my teeth	when he got lost.
b	My teacher was annoyed	after I had been to Italy.
c	The man asked for directions	which was red and juicy.
d	Everyone cheered	before I went to bed.
e	I ate an apple	when I got all my spellings wrong.
f	I visited France	because I scored a goal.
g	I don't like apples	so I only eat bananas.

2 Write the complex sentences you made. Underline the verbs in them.

a ____

b ____

c ____

d ____

e ____

f ____

g ____

Unit 30: Proverbs

Remember

Proverbs are **wise sayings** that have been around for **a long time**. Their **purpose** is to **teach us lessons on how to live**. Sometimes their **meanings** may be **difficult to understand**.

Look before you leap.

This really means:
Don't rush into things. Think carefully before you make any decisions.

Have a go

1. Match the beginning and ending of each of these proverbs:

a	The early bird	are soon parted.
b	New brooms	run deep.
c	A fool and his money	catches the worm.
d	No news	deserves another.
e	Practice	sweep clean.
f	Still waters	makes perfect.
g	One good turn	early to rise.
h	Early to bed,	is good news.

2. Use these words to complete each proverb:

first served	**ends well**	**less speed**	**think alike**
no robbery	**saves nine**	**than never**	**twice shy**

a All's well that ___________________.

b Better late ___________________.

c Fair exchange is ___________________.

d First come, ___________________.

e Once bitten, ___________________.

f Great minds ___________________.

g More haste, ___________________.

h A stitch in time ___________________.

Unit 31: Pronouns (2)

Remember

A **pronoun** is a word that **takes the place of a noun**.
A piece of writing may be written in:

- the **1st person** when it is about **ourselves**: I (singular), we (plural)

- the **2nd person** when it is about **you**: you (may be either singular or plural)

- the **3rd person** when it is about **others**: he, she, it (singular), they (plural)

Have a go

1 Say if the underlined pronoun is singular (S) or plural (P).

a <u>I</u> am going to the shops. (__)

b <u>He</u> is going to school. (__)

c <u>They</u> are going to town. (__)

d <u>She</u> is going on holiday. (__)

e <u>It</u> is going too fast. (__)

f <u>We</u> are going home. (__)

g "Where are <u>you</u> going?" the teacher asked the children. (__)

h "Where are <u>you</u> going?" the teacher asked Ben. (__)

2 Put in the missing pronoun.

a _____ began to rain. (3rd person singular)

b Will _____ pass the salt, please? (2nd person singular)

c _____ love bananas. (1st person singular)

d _____ ran all the way home. (3rd person plural)

e Emma was a nice girl. _____ loved to help. (3rd person singular)

f Ben picked up the bag. _____ looked inside it (3rd person singular)

g "_____ know how to do it," the children shouted. (1st person plural)

h "Stop shouting! _____ are too noisy!" Mrs Jones said. (2nd person plural)

Unit 32: Suffixes

Remember

We add a **suffix** to the **end** of a word to **change its meaning** or **the way it is used**. It may **sometimes** change the **spelling** of the **root** word.

explode + sion = explo**sion**
(verb)   (suffix)   (noun)

Have a go

1 Do these suffix sums. Write the words you make.
   Take care with the spelling.

a beauty + ful = _____________   b happy + ness = _____________

c ignore + ant = _____________   d argue + ment = _____________

e response + ive = _____________   f cycle + ist = _____________

g drum + er = _____________   h wise + dom = _____________

i study + ent = _____________   j prince + ess = _____________

k athlete + ic = _____________   l run + ing = _____________

2 Take the suffix off each word. Write the root word correctly.

a remembrance   **remember**   b baker   _____________

c contractor   _____________   d admission   _____________

e perspiration   _____________   f icicle   _____________

g mountaineer   _____________   h downward   _____________

i kingdom   _____________   j amusement   _____________

k service   _____________   l friendship   _____________

m apologise   _____________   n sparkle   _____________

o breakable   _____________   p magnetise   _____________

Unit 33: Editing sentences

 Remember

When we **edit** our work (reread and correct what we have written) we can sometimes find ways of **shortening** sentences.

The ~~huge, fierce~~ monster came nearer.

The boy stopped. He stopped because he was tired. ~~The boy stopped because he was tired.~~

We can shorten sentences by **leaving out** some words.

We can **combine two sentences** into one.

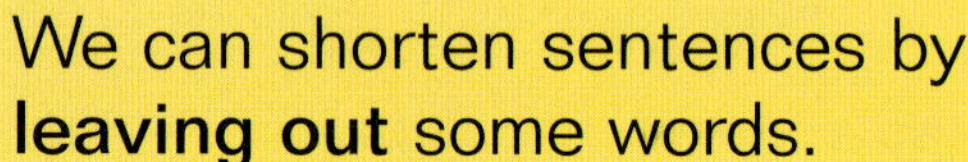 Have a go

1 Shorten these sentences by crossing out all the adjectives and adverbs.

a The small black dog barked noisily at the intruder.
b The grey-haired old lady spoke quietly to her friend.
c The bearded man finished the race easily.
d The young footballer skilfully scored the winning goal.
e Mr Briggs silently slipped out of the back door.
f The attractive actress waited eagerly for the reporter to arrive.
g My new bike was badly damaged in an accident.

2 Combine each of these pairs of sentences into one shorter sentence with the same meaning.

a We will go on a school trip. We will go on it as soon as possible.

____

b The water ran into the drains. It ran into the drains until they overflowed.

____

c My brother is in hospital. He is in hospital to have an operation.

____

d The footballer kicked the ball. He kicked the ball right out of the stadium.

____

e The girl was wet. She was wet because it was raining.

____

f I went to the market. The market is in town.

____

Unit 34: Double negatives

Remember

Standard English is thought of as the 'correct' form of written English used in schools, business and government.

Non-standard English is often used in everyday speech. In non-standard English **double negatives** are often used.

This is in **non-standard** English.

↓

I haven't got no money.

This is in **standard** English.

↓

I haven't got any money.

Have a go

1 Tick the sentences which are correct.
Cross each sentence which contains a double negative.

a I haven't got no football boots. ◯   b That is not right. ◯

c I can't do anything. ◯   d The girl didn't say nothing. ◯

e I never saw nobody. ◯   f I have not seen anyone. ◯

g I have not been anywhere. ◯   h I didn't go nowhere nice. ◯

i There isn't no point going out. ◯   j I don't want any beans. ◯

2 Write each of these sentences correctly.

a He don't know nothing. ______________________________

b I haven't got no money. ______________________________

c I don't want no trouble. ______________________________

d They weren't nowhere near the shop. ______________________________

e I'm not never going swimming again. ______________________________

f The children did not take no notice. ______________________________

g He couldn't find his sister nowhere. ______________________________

h I haven't done nothing wrong. ______________________________

Unit 35: Connectives (2)

Remember

Connectives are words or phrases that can **join** together **ideas** or **sentences**.
A connective may be a **single** word or **more than** one word.

I will put on some clean clothes **as soon as** I get home.

Have a go

1 Match up the beginning and ending of each sentence.
Underline the connective within each sentence.

He was not really hungry	in order to hear it better.
We turned up the TV	after the match finished.
I could not do it	<u>but</u> he still ate a big meal.
The crowd went home	so I did nothing.
If you are naughty	although it was the last one.
I tipped out the water	however hard I tried.
I couldn't decide what to do	then you will get into trouble.
I gave my friend the sweet	until there was none left.

2 Complete each sentence in your own words. Underline the connective in
each sentence.

a We stayed indoors while __________________________.

b I ran out of the room before __________________________.

c The crowd quietened down when __________________________.

d We went out even though __________________________.

e Amy locked the door so that __________________________.

f The test was too hard but __________________________.

g I like to go swimming whenever __________________________.

h My bike got a puncture and so __________________________.

Unit 36: Word origins – Greek

The English language has been influenced by **many other languages**. Many **prefixes** come from the **Greek** language and have a specific meaning. Understanding the **origins** of words sometimes helps us to spell them.

octo means **eight** as in **octopus**

| parallel | microscope | syllable | television | octopus |
| photograph | diameter | hydrofoil | hypermarket | autograph |

1 Write the words from the box in the correct place in the table.

2 Use a dictionary. Look up another word beginning with the same prefix.

Greek prefix	meaning	word from box which begins with the prefix	another word which begins with the same prefix
tele	from afar	television	telephone
photo	light		
hydro	water		
dia	through		
octo	eight		
hyper	over		
para	beside		
syl	together		
auto	self		
micro	small		

Unit 37: Prepositions (2)

Remember

A **preposition** tells us about the **position** of something or someone in relation to someone or something else.
Prepositions are usually placed **in front of nouns** or **pronouns** in sentences.

The girl is hiding **behind** the door.

Have a go

1 Think of a suitable preposition to complete each sentence.

    a I put the book _________ the drawer.

    b The man ran _________ the path.

    c The ball went _________ the window.

    d The speeding car came _________ me.

    e I woke up _________ the night.

    f Electricity cables are laid _________ the ground.

    g She placed the lamp _________ the bed.

    h I went to the cinema _________ my friend.

2 Use the following prepositions in suitable sentences of your own.

    around ____

    down ____

    beside ____

    between ____

    near ____

    upon ____

    above ____

    through ____

Remember

Playing with words can help us learn more about **spelling**

If we change the **and** in st**and** to **are** we can st**and** and st**are**!

Have a go

Make some new words.

a   Instead of **hum** in **hum**our, write **rum**, **col**, **flav**, **lab**.

   rumour __________ __________ __________

b   Instead of **post** in **post**age, write **band**, **vill**, **dam**, **mess**.

   __________ __________ __________ __________

c   Instead of **not** in **not**ice, write **off**, **pol**, **adv**, **just**.

   __________ __________ __________ __________

d   Instead of **ag** in **ag**ain, write **barg**, **expl**, **refr**, **compl**.

   __________ __________ __________ __________

e   Instead of **feat** in de**feat**, write **sire**, **fy**, **clare**, **velop**.

   __________ __________ __________ __________

f   Instead of **op** in gall**op**, write **ey**, **ant**, **ery**, **ows**.

   __________ __________ __________ __________

g   Instead of **cave** in con**cave**, write **duct**, **sider**, **test**, **tain**.

   __________ __________ __________ __________

h   Instead of **bid** in for**bid**, write **sake**, **get**, **give**, **tune**.

   __________ __________ __________ __________

Remember

A **semi-colon** is **stronger** than a **comma** but **not as strong** as a **full stop**. It may be used to **separate parts of a sentence**.

Sam loves cats; Dan prefers dogs.

A **colon** is sometimes used:

* before someone speaks   Sam said: "What's in your bag?"

* to introduce a list   You will need: eggs, jam and bread.

Have a go

1 Fill in the missing semi-colons.

a   I waited patiently soon it would be time to go.
b   Joanne was late home she would be in trouble.
c   Bring me something to eat I'd like some baked beans, please.
d   He was freezing the water was very icy.
e   Come in, please explain what has happened.
f   Tom loves Indian food Matthew prefers Chinese food.
g   The cake was very pleasant it tasted delicious.
h   The woods were quiet the only sound was the rustle of the wind in the trees.

2 Fill in the missing colons.

a   The king stood up and said "I've lost my crown."
b   See what's in the box books, magazines and comics.
c   The explorer roared "Look out!"
d   The Prime Minister stood up and said "Taxes will have to be raised."
e   Outside there were farm animals horses, sheep and cows.
f   You will need pencils, paper and a ruler.
g   Dan shouted "Pass me the ball!"
h   Bring these for your ski trip your passport, a woolly hat and some gloves.

Unit 40: Dictionary work – definitions

Remember

Dictionaries help us to find out the
definitions (meanings) of words.

a **boy** was holding onto a **buoy**

boy	a male child
buoy	a floating warning marker for boats at sea

Have a go

Write definitions for each of these pairs of homophones.
Use a dictionary to help you.

a aisle ____

b isle ____

c berry ____

d bury ____

e currant ____

f current ____

g faint ____

h feint ____

i idle ____

j idol ____

k key ____

l quay ____

m main ____

n mane ____

o paws ____

p pause ____

q steel ____

r steal ____

Test 1

Check how much you have learned.

Answer the questions.
Mark your answers. Fill in your score.

1 Underline the common letter patterns in these sets of words:

a wedge   budge   ridge

b hutch   stitch   catch

out of 2

2 Fill in the missing verbs.

verb	present tense	past tense	future tense
draw	I am drawing	I ___________	I will draw
sleep	I am sleeping	I ___________	I will sleep

out of 2

3 Choose **ure** or **our** to complete each word.

a harb_______   b treas_______

out of 2

4 Write the plural of each noun.

a thief ___________   b lorry ___________

out of 2

5 Choose the best adjective to complete each simile.

quiet   slippery

a as _________ as an eel

b as _________ as a mouse

out of 2

6 Add the suffix. Write each word correctly.

a nose + y = __________

b ice + y = __________

7 Underline the adverb in each sentence.

a I waited patiently for the bus.

b Reluctantly I walked home when it didn't come.

8 Choose the correct letter to begin each word.

a 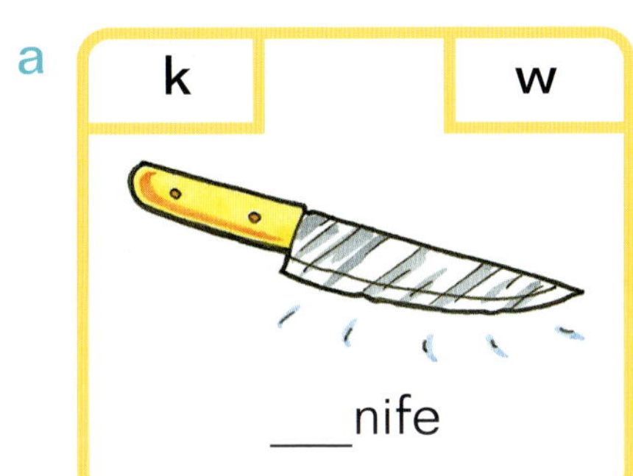

b 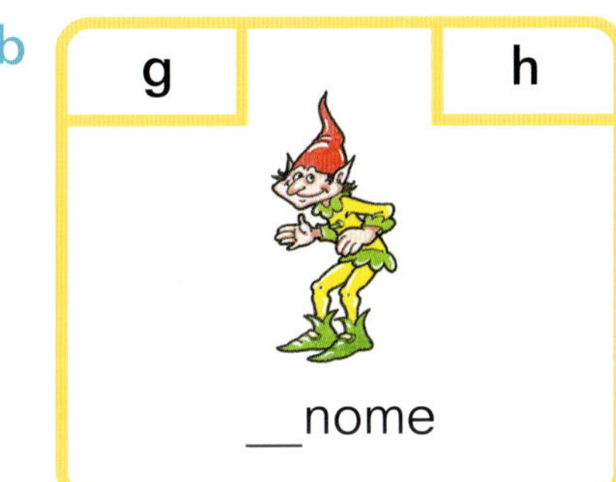

9 Underline the subject and circle the verb in this one-clause sentence:

The guard dog slept in the kennel outside.

10 Write which word each Cockney rhyming slang phrase stands for.

stairs   sister

a skin and blister __________

b apples and pears __________

Check how much you have learned.

Answer the questions.
Mark your answers. Fill in your score.

SCORE

1 Write what the underlined pronoun in each sentence stands for.

  a Sam sat down when <u>he</u> (_____) got home.

  b The birds flew away when <u>they</u> (_____) saw the cat.

out of 2

2 Choose the correct prefix to begin each word.

a

super	sub

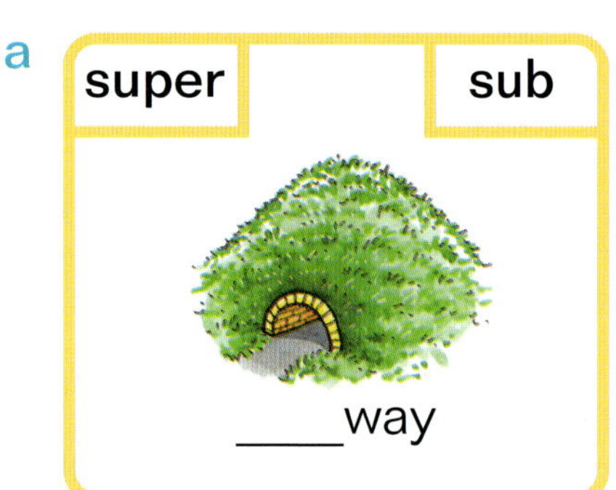

____way

b

em	ex

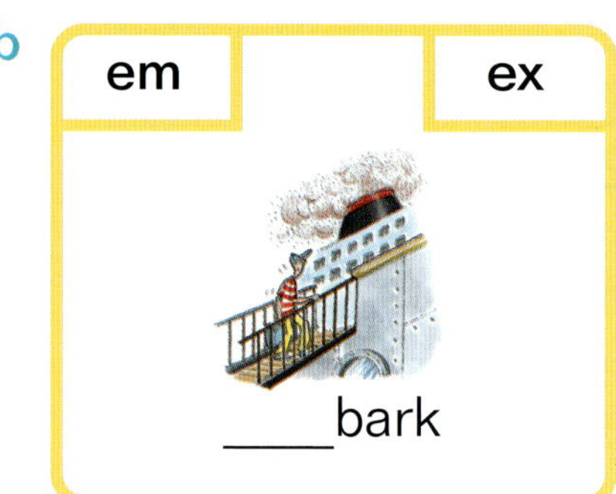

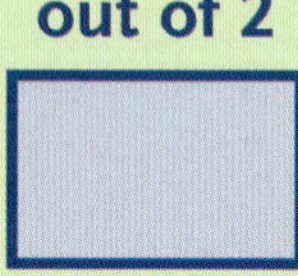

____bark

out of 2

3 Rewrite each sentence. Begin it with the adverb.

  a The sun shone brightly. ___________________

  b I ran home quickly. ___________________

out of 2

4 Rewrite each sentence in standard English.

  a Where you going? ___________________

  b Me and Paul are going to play cricket.

____

out of 2

5 Underline the connective in each sentence.

  a I went to the library because I wanted a book.

  b I kept reading until I was tired.

out of 2

6 Tick the word you think comes from each Latin root word.

a **videre (to look)** → avoid ☐
                   → evident ☐

b **signum (sign)** → signal ☐
                  → cigar ☐

out of 2

7 Underline the preposition in each sentence.

a The ball was under the table.

b I was pushed against the wall.

out of 2

8 Write the words you are left with:

a Take **rest** out of **restart** __________

b Take **arm** out of **farmed** __________

out of 2

9 Fill in the missing pair of brackets.

The Eiffel Tower a metal structure is in Paris.

out of 2

10 Write these words in alphabetical order:

become **beware** **befriend** **because**

__________ __________ __________ __________

out of 2

Total out of 20

Test 3

1 Do these syllable sums. Write the words you make.

   a   rob + ber + y = __________

   b   con + tent + ment = __________

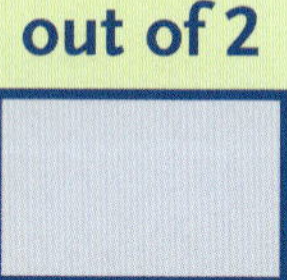

2 Rewrite these sentences.
Change the verbs from the passive to the active.

   a   The tree was climbed by the girl.

      ____

   b   The apple was eaten by the boy

      ____

3 Complete each word with either **ant** or **ent**.

   a   extravag______   b   intellig______

4 Say whether the gender of each noun in the sentence is
masculine (m), feminine (f), common (c) or neuter (n).

       The woman (___) sat on the chair (___).

5 Match each compound adjective with its meaning.

     light-fingered   **green-fingered**

   a   Someone who is good at gardening is __________.

   b   Someone who steals is __________.

6 Choose **ie** or **ei** to complete each word.

a

sh_____ld

b

c_____ling

out of 2

7 Write whether each word is:

- an adverb of manner (M)

- an adverb of time (T)

- an adverb of place (P).

a soon (___)

b everywhere (___)

out of 2

8 Spell each word correctly.

a chargable ________________

b servicable ________________

out of 2

9 Underline the verbs in these sentences.
Say how many clauses there are in each sentence.

a The thunder roared and the rain fell
heavily. (___)

b The old man sat down tiredly. (___)

out of 2

10 Choose the correct ending for each proverb.

than never   **deserves another**

a One good turn __________________________.

b Better late __________________________.

out of 2

Total out of 20

Test 4

Check how much you have learned.

Answer the questions.
Mark your answers. Fill in your score.

1 Say if the underlined pronouns are singular (S) or plural (P).

They (___) were lost but I (___) had a map.

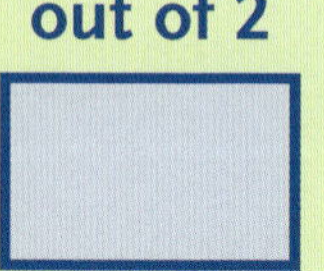

2 Add the suffix to each word. Spell the word you make correctly.

a inspire + ing = ________________

b educate + tion = ________________

3 Shorten this sentence by crossing out the adjective and the adverb.

 The naughty monkey ate the banana greedily.

4 Write each sentence in standard English.

a I don't know nothing.

____

b He didn't have no money.

____

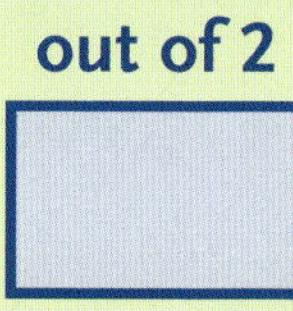

5 Underline the connectives in these sentences.

a I unlocked the box so that I could look inside.

b I watch TV whenever I can.

6 Tick the word you think comes from each Greek root word.

a **graph (to write)** → biography ☐

→ laugh ☐

b **aster (star)** → ask ☐

→ asteroid ☐

out of 2

7 Fill in the missing letters in these prepositions.

a ar _ _ nd   b be _ _ _ d

out of 2

8 Make some new words:

Instead of **cry** in de**cry** write: **a ride**   **b cipher**

a ______________   b ______________

out of 2

9 Fill in the missing colon or semi-colon in each sentence.

a Don't go away I want to talk to you.

b The bag contained the following apples, pears, grapes and bananas.

out of 2

10 Use a dictionary. Write definitions for:

a pane ______________________________

b pain ______________________________

out of 2

Total out of 20

Unit 1: Looking for letter patterns   There are a number of strategies your child can learn to help him or her spell better. Looking for common letter patterns in groups of words, and using these patterns to create other words is one such useful strategy.

Unit 2: Revising verb tenses   Verbs may be written in different tenses. When a verb tells of an action taking place now, we say that it is written in the present tense e.g. I am riding my bike. A verb describing action which has already taken place is written in the past tense e.g. Last week I bought a new car. A verb describing something that will happen in the future is written in the future tense e.g. Tomorrow I will go to town.

Unit 3: Word endings – *ure* and *our*   There are many common word endings. It is important for your child to recognise these when reading and to be able to use them when writing. The common word endings **ure** and **our** (which often sound the same) are the focus of this unit.

Unit 4: Nouns – singular and plural   Remind your child that nouns (naming words) may be singular (when there is only one) or plural (when there is more than one). The most usual way of showing the plural form is to add **s**. However, this is not always the case by any means! This unit focuses on various ways of pluralising nouns.

Unit 5: Similes   Remind your child that an adjective is a describing word which tells us more about a noun. We often use similes to compare one thing with another e.g. The man was as strong as an ox. Similes often include adjectives, which are the focus of the activities in this unit.

Unit 6: Spelling rules (1)   Much of our spelling system is governed by logical rules. Understanding these can help your child develop sound spelling strategies. The spelling rule focused on here is that when we add **y** to a word ending in **e**, we drop the **e** before adding the **y** e.g. ice + **y** = icy.

Unit 7: Adverbs (1)   Remind your child that an adverb tells us more about a verb. Many adverbs (adverbs of manner) tell us about how something happened. Many of these adverbs end with the suffix **ly**.

Unit 8: Silent letters   Some words contain silent letters (which we cannot hear when we say the words) e.g. wrap. Words beginning with the silent letters **k** e.g. know, **g** e.g. gnome and **w** e.g. wriggle are dealt with in this unit.

Unit 9: Clauses (1)   A clause is a group of words which may be used as a whole sentence, or as part of a sentence. A clause must contain a verb (a doing word) and have a subject (the person or thing that the verb refers to). An example of a one-clause sentence is: The spacecraft (subject) landed (verb) on the moon. Identifying the verbs in a sentence is a good way of working out how many clauses the sentence contains.

Unit 10: Common expressions   In different areas of the country people have different ways of saying the same things. This use of words or grammar is called a dialect. Many people from the East End of London, often called Cockneys, have developed a dialect called Cockney rhyming slang. For example, in Cockney rhyming slang 'loaf of bread' really means 'head'. This unit introduces your child to some common expressions in Cockney rhyming slang.

Unit 11: Pronouns (1)   Remind your child that a pronoun is a word that takes the place of a noun. ('Pro' actually means 'in place of'.) We use pronouns to avoid a lot of repetition in sentences. Personal pronouns take the place of the names of people or things, for example, Tom bought a comic when he (Tom) went out. Possessive pronouns show us who or what owns something e.g. This book is mine.

Unit 12: Prefixes   A prefix is a group of letters we can add to the front of a word. Prefixes change the meaning of the word. A variety of different prefixes are featured in this unit.

Unit 13: Word order in sentences   Sometimes the order in which words are arranged is crucial to the meaning. By changing the order of some words, meaning may be destroyed e.g. 'The cake baked the lady'. However, this is not always the case. The activities in this unit show how the reporting phrase in dialogue can either come at the beginning or end of a sentence (e.g. "I'm lost," the boy exclaimed means the same as <u>The boy exclaimed, "I'm lost."</u>). Also we can sometimes move an adverb around without affecting the meaning of the sentence (e.g. The boy crept <u>quietly</u> into the room. <u>Quietly</u> the boy crept into the room.).

Unit 14: Standard English   Standard English is the kind of language your child is expected to use in school. We often use non-standard English informally when speaking. This unit encourages your child to identify differences between standard and non-standard English.

Unit 15: Connectives (1)   Connectives are words or phrases that can join together ideas or sentences. A connective may be a single word or more than one word e.g. Sarah was out of breath, <u>but nevertheless</u> (a two-word connective) she still kept running.

Unit 16: Word origins – Latin   The English language has been influenced by many other languages. Understanding the origins of words is interesting in its own right but may also help us to understand the spelling of them. Many English words have their roots in Latin, the language of the Romans. For example, in Latin 'audio' means 'I hear' from which we get the words 'audience', 'auditorium', 'auditory' etc.

Unit 17: Prepositions (1)   Remind your child that prepositions often tell us about the position of one thing in relation to another. They are usually to be found in front of nouns in sentences e.g. The train went <u>through</u> the tunnel.

Unit 18: Fun with words   Spelling is very much a visual skill. Being able to see smaller words 'hiding' inside longer words is helpful in learning how to spell the longer word. However, when we take out the smaller word we are sometimes left with another meaningful word, as the activity in this unit demonstrates.

Unit 19: Dashes and brackets   Two fairly sophisticated punctuation marks are introduced in this unit – the dash (stronger than a comma – but not as strong as a full stop) and parenthetic brackets (used to enclose information to separate it from the rest of the sentence – like the brackets in this example!).

Unit 20: Alphabetical order   Many books are arranged in alphabetical order e.g. dictionaries, encyclopedia etc. This unit focuses on understanding and using alphabetical order.

Unit 21: Syllables   Breaking words down into syllables is a helpful spelling strategy. When we say words slowly we can hear how they may be broken down into smaller parts, called syllables. It is helpful to tap or clap these 'beats' when saying words to help emphasise the syllables.

Unit 22: Active and passive verbs   Verbs may be written in different forms. In this unit the active and passive forms of verbs are studied. A verb is active when the subject performs the action e.g. The girl <u>ate</u> the cake. A verb is passive when the subject of the sentence has the action done to it e.g. The cake <u>was eaten</u> by the girl. The passive form of the verb is often used in reporting events e.g. in newspapers.

Unit 23: Word endings – *ant* and *ent*   The common word endings **ant** and **ent** (which often sound the same) are the focus of this unit.

Unit 24: Nouns – gender   Nouns may be classified according to their gender. Nouns which refer to males (e.g. king) are masculine. Nouns which refer to females (e.g. queen) are feminine. Nouns which may refer to either males or females have a common gender (e.g. baby). Nouns without gender are said to be neuter (e.g. chair).

Unit 25: Compound adjectives   Compound adjectives are made up of two words, often joined together by a hyphen e.g. light-headed. Hyphens help make the meaning clearer e.g. I saw a man-eating tiger. I saw a man eating tiger!

Unit 26: Spelling rules (2)   The spelling rule focused on in this unit is one of the most well-known and quoted rules. It reminds children always to put **i** (when it makes the sound **ee** as in 'believe') before **e** except after **c**.

Unit 27: Adverbs (2)   There are different types of adverb. Adverbs of manner tell us *how* something happened. Many of these adverbs end in **ly** e.g. quickly. Adverbs of time tell us *when* something happened e.g. He came **later**. Adverbs of place tell us *where* something happened e.g. He came **here**.

Unit 28: Tricky spellings   When adding a suffix beginning with **a** or **o** after a 'soft' **c** or **g**, we always retain the 'silent' **e** at the end of the word to keep the **c** or **g** soft e.g. notic**e** + able = notic**e**able; courage + ous = courag**e**ous.

Unit 29: Clauses (2)   A clause must contain a verb (a doing word) and have a subject (the person or thing that the verb refers to). Identifying the verbs in a sentence is a good way of working out how many clauses the sentence contains e.g. I <u>picked</u> some flowers (clause 1) which <u>grew</u> in my garden (clause 2). (This is an example of a two-clause sentence, each clause having its own verb.)

Unit 30: Proverbs   This unit introduces proverbs, which are wise sayings that have been around for a long time. Their purpose is to teach us lessons on how to live. Sometimes their meanings may be difficult to understand. For example 'Look before you leap' really means 'Don't rush into things. Think carefully before you make any decisions.'

Unit 31: Pronouns (2)   Pronouns may be written in the 1st person when we write about ourselves (e.g. I, me, we, us). 2nd person pronouns are used when we write to others (e.g. you). We use 3rd person pronouns (e.g. he, she, it, they) when we write about others. Pronouns may be singular (when they stand for one person or thing e.g. she) or plural (when they stand for more than one person or thing e.g. they).

Unit 32: Suffixes   A suffix is a group of letters we add to the end of a word. Your child needs to understand that many words may be extended by adding suffixes. Adding a suffix changes the meaning or function of the word in some way e.g. explode (verb) + sion (suffix) = explosion (noun).

Unit 33: Editing sentences   Some sentences may be shortened by leaving out some types of words. For example, we can leave out the adjectives in a sentence without affecting the meaning too much: The ~~huge, fierce~~ monster came nearer. However, there are some types of words we could not leave out e.g. the verb: The huge, fierce monster ~~came~~ nearer.

Unit 34: Double negatives   In non-standard English grammatically incorrect sentences are sometimes spoken. Double negatives are often used e.g. I never saw nobody.

Unit 35: Connectives (2)   A connective may be a single word or more than one word e.g. Sarah was out of breath, <u>but nevertheless</u> (a two-word connective) she still kept running.

Unit 36: Word origins – Greek   Many English words have their roots in Greek. For example, the Greek prefix 'octo' means 'eight' as in 'octopus'.

Unit 37: Prepositions (2)   This unit provides further work on prepositions, as studied in Unit 17.

Unit 38: Fun with words (2)   Encouraging your child to play and experiment with words is a good way to help them to learn more about spelling. The activities in this unit do just this.

Unit 39: Colons and semi-colons   Two fairly sophisticated punctuation marks are introduced in this unit. The semi-colon (;) is stronger than a comma but not as strong as a full stop. It may be used to separate or 'balance' two parts of a sentence (e.g. Sam loves cats; Dan prefers dogs). A colon (:) is sometimes used before someone speaks (e.g. The king said: "Where's my crown?"). It is also sometimes used to introduce a list (e.g. For skiing you need: some skis, ski boots, goggles, a waterproof anorak and trousers.).

Unit 40: Dictionary work – definitions   Your child needs to know how to use a dictionary effectively. This unit focuses on its function of providing definitions for words. It asks your child to explain the difference between pairs of homophones (words which sound alike but have different meanings such as 'boy' and 'buoy').

Answers

Unit 1: Looking for letter patterns (page 6)

'dom' words
boredom
freedom
kingdom

'tion' words
examination
education
conversation

'ch' words
choir
character
chemist

'au' words
pause
saucer
author

'ear' words
learn
search
early

'edge' words
hedge
ledge
wedge

Unit 2: Revising verb tenses (page 7)

1

verb	present tense	past tense	future tense
dig	I am digging	I dug	I will dig
break	I am breaking	I broke	I will break
driving	I am driving	I drove	I will drive
fly	I am flying	I flew	I will fly
push	I am pushing	I pushed	I will push
sit	I am sitting	I sat	I will sit
write	I am writing	I wrote	I will write
sleep	I am sleeping	I slept	I will sleep

2
a Tom will go to the shed.
b He will put on his boots.
c Tom will pick up a fork.
d He will dig the garden.

Unit 3: Word endings – *ure* and *our* (page 8)

1
a nat**ure**   fail**ure**   fig**ure**
  treas**ure**   meas**ure**
b col**our**   arm**our**   fav**our**
  hon**our**   harb**our**

2
fixture   neighbour
creature   moisture
rumour   fracture
splendour   structure
vigour   flavour

Unit 4: Nouns – singular and plural (page 9)

The second examples for each of the rules are suggestions only. Many other answers are possible.

singular	plural
a cat	cats
pillow	**pillows**
b tray	**trays**
boy	**boys**
c lady	ladies
berry	**berries**
d bush	bushes
church	**churches**
e knife	knives
loaf	**loaves**
f tomato	tomatoes
potato	**potatoes**
g radio	radios
cameo	**cameos**
h sheep	sheep
cannon	**cannon**

Unit 5: Similes (page 10)

1
a blind   b gentle   c sharp
d hot   e slippery   f thin
g flat   h wise   i fit
j keen

2 The answers given are examples. Other answers are possible.

a small   b gentle   c solid
d rough   e quiet   f brave
g dry   h smooth   i fast
j wet   k light   l soft

Unit 6: Spelling rules (1) (page 11)

1
a icy   b lacy   c stony
d noisy   e breezy   f edgy
g smoky   h wiry   i juicy
j lazy   k shady   l hazy

2 breezy, edgy, hazy, icy, juicy, lacy, lazy, noisy, shady, smoky, stony, wiry

3 smoke, juice, haze, ice, stone, laze, shade, wire, breeze, edge, lace, noise

Unit 7: Adverbs (1) (page 12)

1
a The woman laughed happily.
b The cat sat quietly on the mat.
c In the exam, the boy wrote quickly.
d The knight fought bravely.
e The people in the queue waited patiently.
f Sam wearily plodded home.
g Suddenly the door opened.
h The footballer skilfully dribbled past his opponent.

2

verbs	adverbs
fight	aimlessly
arrive	fluently
wander	heroically
wait	awkwardly
speak	punctually
give	faithfully
fall	patiently
promise	generously

Unit 8: Silent letters (page 13)

1

a **k**now   b **g**nu   c **w**reck

d **g**narled   e **k**not   f **w**rite

g **k**neel   h **w**rap   i **w**riggle

j **g**nat   k **k**nuckle   l **w**rinkle

2

gnu — to get down on your knees

know — a large African antelope

wreck — to put words on paper for people to read

gnarled — to understand and remember something

knot — to damage something so it cannot be used again

write — one of the places where your fingers bend

kneel — twisted like the trunk of an old tree

wrap — the twisted part where something has been tied together

wriggle — to twist and turn the body like a worm

gnat — a small crease in the skin

knuckle — a small fly that bites

wrinkle — to put cloth or paper round something

Unit 9: Clauses (1) (page 14)

1

a The monkey pulled a funny face.

b The girl walked over the bridge.

c The children entered the museum.

d Toby scored the winning goal.

e Sharks swim in the sea.

f The dinosaur roared loudly.

g We found a crab in the rockpool.

h Pandas eat bamboo shoots.

2

a I like Saturdays because we go to town. (2)

b The fox hunted for food in the forest. (1)

c The sun shone and the wind blew. (2)

d I ate curry and rice hungrily. (1)

e The story started in an exciting manner. (1)

f Lions show their teeth when they roar. (2)

g I bought a comic when the shop opened. (2)

h The old lady drove very fast. (1)

Unit 10: Common expressions (page 15)

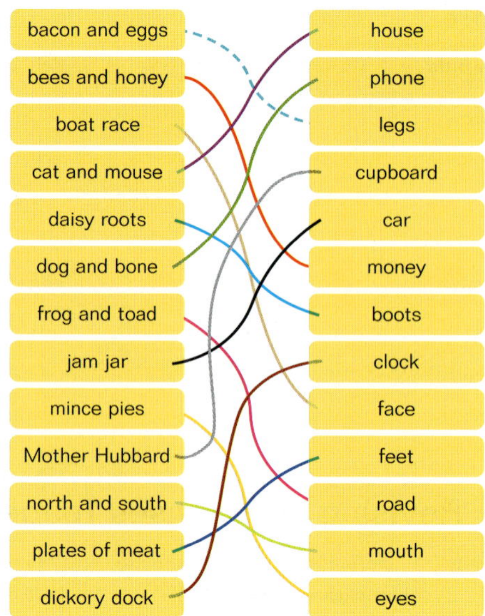

bacon and eggs	house
bees and honey	phone
boat race	legs
cat and mouse	cupboard
daisy roots	car
dog and bone	money
frog and toad	boots
jam jar	clock
mince pies	face
Mother Hubbard	feet
north and south	road
plates of meat	mouth
dickory dock	eyes

Unit 11: Pronouns (1) (page 16)

1

a James/the pencil

b Sophie/the TV

c Mr Jones

d Amy and Emily

e the trousers/the man

f the cows/the girl

g the alien

h Jenny

2

a mine   b hers

c his   d ours

e yours   f theirs/mine

Unit 12: Prefixes (page 17)

1

a **anti**clockwise   b **be**friend

c **centi**metre   d **de**fend

e **ex**change   f **im**patient

g **mid**day   h **multi**purpose

i **over**cast   j **pre**arrange

k **sub**marine   l **trans**port

2

a theatre   b ability

c circle   d change

e tell   f sphere

g active   h port

i metre   j night

k judge   l sense

m balance   n date

o mount   p hill

Unit 13: Word order in sentences (page 18)

1
a The children shouted, "Come quickly!"
b Tom called, "I'm going out."
c The man said, "The grass needs cutting."
d Sam asked, "Can I come with you?"
e Harry moaned, "I want a drink."
f Mary asked, "Have you seen my bag?"

2
a The explorer faced the lion <u>bravely</u>.
  Bravely the explorer faced the lion.
b Anna wrote in her book <u>neatly</u>.
  Neatly Anna wrote in her book.
c The children whispered together <u>quietly</u>.
  Quietly the children whispered together.
d I read the question <u>slowly</u>.
  Slowly I read the question.
e The car appeared <u>suddenly</u>.
  Suddenly the car appeared.
f I slammed the door <u>noisily</u>.
  Noisily I slammed the door.

Unit 14: Standard English (page 19)

1
a Sam and I watched television. ✓
b Who has got my pencil? ✓
c They are coming soon. ✓
d I did not see anything. ✓
e I am not going anywhere. ✓
f What are you staring at? ✓
g We were just going out. ✓
h Here are the sweets that I bought. ✓

2
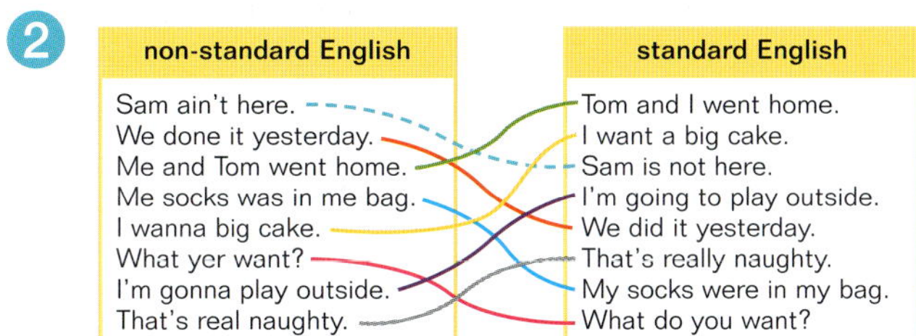

Unit 15: Connectives (1) (page 20)

1
a <u>so</u>
b <u>if</u>
c <u>because</u>
d <u>although</u>
e <u>before</u>
f <u>therefore</u>
g <u>while</u>
h <u>whereas</u>

2
a so that
b whenever
c before
d when
e or
f until
g so
h when

Unit 16: Word origins – Latin (page 21)

1
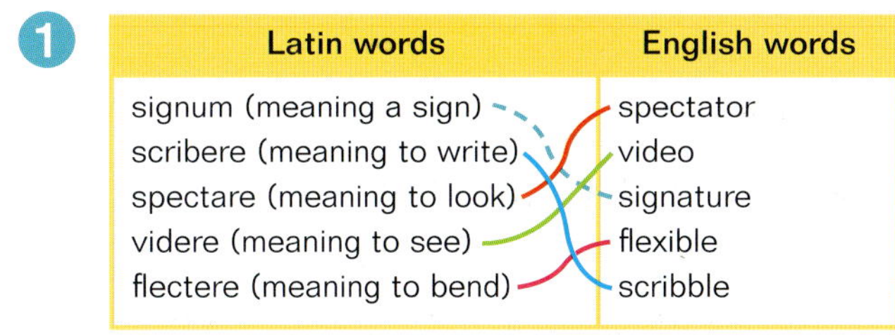

2

'aqua' meaning 'water'	'audio' meaning 'I hear'	'scribo' meaning 'I write'	'circa' meaning 'about'	'primus' meaning 'first'
aqualung	audience	describe	circular	prime
aquaplane	audible	scribble	circuit	primary
aquarium	auditorium	manuscript	circumference	primate

Unit 17: Prepositions (1) (page 22)

1
a <u>in</u>
b <u>at</u>
c <u>across</u>
d <u>behind</u>
e <u>through</u>
f <u>over</u>
g <u>under</u>
h <u>during</u>

2
a between
b past
c into
d behind
e along
f through
g against
h around

Unit 18: Fun with words (1) (page 23)

longer word	word to take out	shorter word left
basket	ask	bet
capable	cap	able
surface	surf	ace
blade	lad	be
bargain	gain	bar
paint	in	pat
mallet	all	met
balanced	lance	bad
threading	read	thing
before	for	bee
garages	rage	gas
father	the	far
snowing	now	sing
money	one	my
feared	ear	fed
slowly	owl	sly
wanted	ant	wed
colossal	loss	coal
puppies	pup	pies

Unit 19: Dashes and brackets (page 24)

1
I bought some fruit – sausage and chips.
My sister loves cabbage – 'The Haunted House'.
It was my favourite meal – a bunch of bananas.
At school Amy won a cup – Liverpool.
I saw a scary film on TV – I hate it!
Hand in your work on Monday – one was very scruffy.
I saw my favourite team – at the latest!
One man was dressed smartly – Best Sportsgirl Cup.

2
a G deciduous trees
b H a bird of prey
c A a football team
d E London
e C five interlinking rings
f D Mount Kilimanjaro
g F December 31st
h B a famous writer

Unit 20: Alphabetical order (page 25)

a behalf behave behind behold
b handbag handcuff handiwork handwriting
c subscribe subsequent subside substitute
d golden goldfish goldmine goldsmith
e transact transfer translate transmit
f collaborate collapse collect college

Unit 21: Syllables (page 26)

1
a conductor
b punishment
c introduce
d insulting
e carefully
f transported
g disappear
h reflection
i signature
j liberty

2
a ac**ro**bat
b lem**on**ade
c Sep**tem**ber
d pro**po**sal
e **u**niform
f es**tab**lish
g hos**pit**al
h at**ten**tion
i dis**cov**er
j help**less**ness or help**ful**ness
k ten**der**ly
l ex**er**tion

Unit 22: Active and passive verbs (page 27)

1

active form	passive form
The boy painted the picture.	A bag was carried by the woman.
The pirate waved a sword.	Some seeds were planted by the man.
The woman carried a bag.	The nuts were hidden by the squirrel.
Sam read a book.	A book was read by Sam.
The man planted some seeds.	A sword was waved by the pirate.
The squirrel hid the nuts.	The picture was painted by the boy.

2
a The car crossed over the bridge.
b Roald Dahl wrote many books.
c The burglar broke into the house.
d Soldiers guarded the palace.
e Mr Griggs opened the can of beans.

Unit 23: Word endings – *ant* and *ent* (page 28)

1
arrog**ant**   obedi**ent**
abund**ant**   intellig**ent**
extravag**ant**   magnific**ent**
ignor**ant**   viol**ent**
fragr**ant**   evid**ent**

2
a obedient
b evident
c extravagant
d magnificent
e fragrant
f abundant
g ignorant
h arrogant
i violent
j intelligent

3
a assist**ant**
b mut**ant**
c abs**ent**
d import**ant**
e eleg**ant**
f sil**ent**
g differ**ent**
h dist**ant**
i defi**ant**
j conveni**ent**

Unit 24: Nouns – gender (page 29)

1

masculine	feminine	common	neuter
husband	niece	pupil	fork
uncle	nun	guest	camera
bull	bride	traveller	hotel
prince	lioness	doctor	car
		friend	
		patient	

2

description	answer	gender
a woman in charge of a school	headmistress	f
a child whose parents are dead	orphan	c
a son of a king	prince	m
the place where prisoners are kept	prison	n
the opposite of a daughter	son	m
someone who writes books	author	c
a utensil you use to cut food	knife	n
the daughter of a queen	princess	f

Unit 25: Compound adjectives (page 30)

1
a angry-looking
b ice-cold
c well-known
d clean-shaven
e long-haired
f three-wheeled
g pet-loving
h light-headed
i hard-working
j football-mad
k shabby-looking
l light-fingered

2
a well-known
b football-mad
c shabby-looking
d hard-working
e long-haired
f light-fingered
g ice-cold
h three-wheeled
i angry-looking
j pet-loving
k clean-shaven
l light-headed

Unit 26: Spelling rules (2) (page 31)

1
th**ie**f f**ie**ld sh**ie**ld p**ie**ce n**ie**ce
br**ie**f f**ie**rce p**ie**rce ach**ie**ve bel**ie**ve

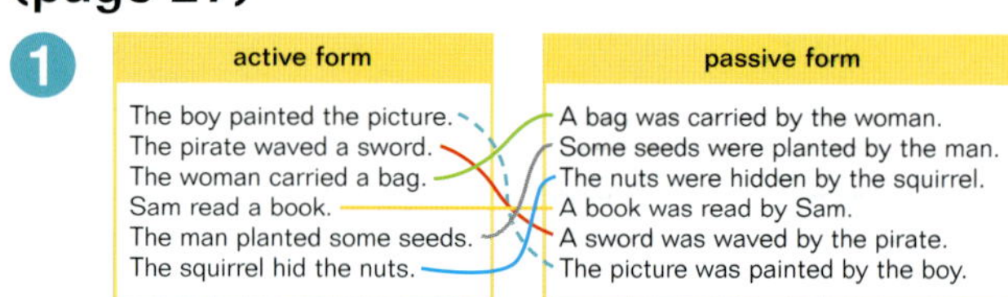

2
a shr**ie**k b rec**ei**ve
c pr**ie**st d c**ei**ling
e misch**ie**f f p**ie**ce
g dec**ei**ve h sh**ie**ld
i rel**ie**f j conc**ei**t
k y**ie**ld l bel**ie**ve
m rec**ei**pt n gr**ie**f
o perc**ei**ve

3

ie words	ei words
shriek	receive
priest	ceiling
mischief	deceive
piece	conceit
shield	receipt
relief	perceive
yield	
believe	
grief	

Unit 27: Adverbs (2) (page 32)

1
a Mrs Smith answered <u>sharply</u>. (M)
b Our visitors arrived <u>yesterday</u>. (T)
c Will you be <u>there</u>? (P)
d We <u>seldom</u> see each other. (T)
e I turned the box <u>around</u>. (P)
f I slept very <u>badly</u>. (M)
g <u>Tomorrow</u> I am going swimming. (T)
h We looked <u>everywhere</u> for the key. (P)

2 Personal answers.

Unit 28: Tricky spellings (page 33)

1
a traceable b noticeable
c changeable d manageable
e courageous f advantageous
g peaceable h serviceable
i chargeable j enforceable
k replaceable l outrageous

2

able words	ous words
traceable	courageous
noticeable	advantageous
changeable	outrageous
manageable	
peaceable	
serviceable	
chargeable	
enforceable	
replaceable	

Unit 29: Clauses (2) (page 34)

1
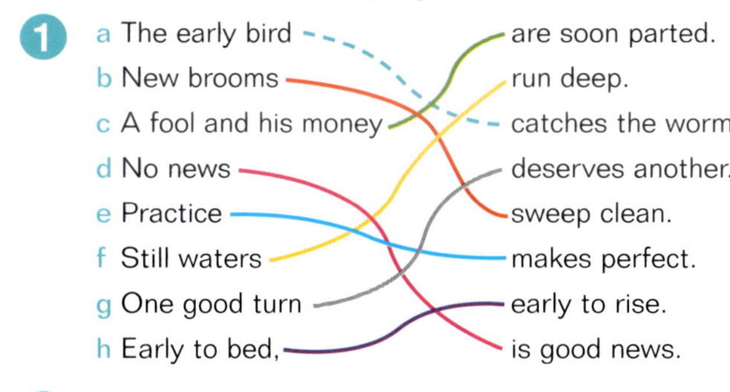

2
a I <u>cleaned</u> my teeth before I <u>went</u> to bed.
b My teacher <u>was</u> annoyed when I <u>got</u> all my spellings wrong.
c The man <u>asked</u> for directions when he <u>got</u> lost.
d Everyone <u>cheered</u> because I <u>scored</u> a goal.
e I <u>ate</u> an apple which <u>was</u> red and juicy.
f I <u>visited</u> France after I <u>had been</u> to Italy.
g I <u>don't like</u> apples so I only <u>eat</u> bananas.

Unit 30: Proverbs (page 35)

1

2
a ends well b than never
c no robbery d first served
e twice shy f think alike
g less speed h saves nine

Unit 31: Pronouns (2) (page 36)

1
a S b S c P d S
e S f P g P h S

2
a It b you c I d They
e She f He g We h You

Unit 32: Suffixes (page 37)

1
a beautiful b happiness
c ignorant d argument
e responsive f cyclist
g drummer h wisdom

i student
j princess
k athletic
l running

2
a remember
b bake
c contract
d admit
e perspire
f ice
g mountain
h down
i king
j amuse
k serve
l friend
m apology
n spark
o break
p magnet

Unit 33: Editing sentences (page 38)

1
a The ~~small black~~ dog barked ~~noisily~~ at the intruder.
b The ~~grey haired old~~ lady spoke ~~quietly~~ to her friend.
c The ~~bearded~~ man finished the race ~~easily~~.
d The ~~young~~ footballer ~~skilfully~~ scored the ~~winning~~ goal.
e Mr Briggs ~~silently~~ slipped out of the ~~back~~ door.
f The ~~attractive~~ actress waited ~~eagerly~~ for the reporter to arrive.
g My ~~new~~ bike was ~~badly~~ damaged in an accident.

2
a We will go on a school trip as soon as possible.
b The water ran into the drains until they overflowed.
c My brother is in hospital to have an operation.
d The footballer kicked the ball right out of the stadium.
e The girl was wet because it was raining.
f I went to the market in town.

Unit 34: Double negatives (page 39)

1
a I haven't got no football boots. ✗
b That is not right. ✓
c I can't do anything. ✓
d The girl didn't say nothing. ✗
e I never saw nobody. ✗
f I have not seen anyone. ✓
g I have not been anywhere. ✓
h I didn't go nowhere nice. ✗
i There isn't no point going out. ✗
j I don't want any beans. ✓

2 Other answers are possible.
a He doesn't know anything.
b I haven't got any money.
c I don't want any trouble.
d They weren't anywhere near the shop.
e I'm never going swimming again.
f The children did not take any notice.
g He couldn't find his sister anywhere.
h I haven't done anything wrong.

Unit 35: Connectives (2) (page 40)

1
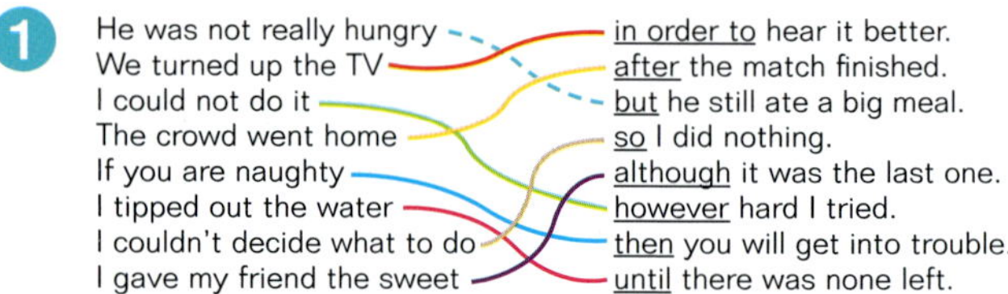

2 The completed answers are examples only. Other answers are possible.
a We stayed indoors <u>while</u> it was raining.
b I ran out of the room <u>before</u> my TV programme was finished.
c The crowd quietened down <u>when</u> the game started.
d We went out <u>even though</u> it was very cold.
e Amy locked the door <u>so that</u> no one could come in.
f The test was too hard <u>but</u> I did quite well.
g I like to go swimming <u>whenever</u> I get the chance.
h My bike got a puncture <u>and so</u> I had to mend it.

Unit 36: Word origins – Greek (page 41)

1 and **2** (Other answers are possible in column 4.)

Greek prefix	meaning	word from box which begins with the prefix	another word which begins with the same prefix
tele	from afar	television	telephone
photo	light	photograph	photosynthesis
hydro	water	hydrofoil	hydrogen
dia	through	diameter	diagnose
octo	eight	octopus	October
hyper	over	hypermarket	hyperactive
para	beside	parallel	parachute
syl	together	syllable	syllabus
auto	self	autograph	automatic
micro	small	microscope	microchip

Unit 37: Prepositions (2) (page 42)

1 The answers given are examples. Other answers are possible.

a in
b along
c through
d past
e during
f under
g beside
h with

2 Many answers are possible. Check that the prepositions have been used correctly in sensible sentences.

Unit 38: Fun with words (2) (page 43)

a rumour   colour   flavour   labour
b bandage   village   damage   message
c office   police   advice   justice
d bargain   explain   refrain   complain
e desire   defy   declare   develop
f galley   gallant   gallery   gallows
g conduct   consider   contest   contain
h forsake   forget   forgive   fortune

Unit 39: Colons and semi-colons (page 44)

1
a I waited patiently; soon it would be time to go.
b Joanne was late home; she would be in trouble.
c Bring me something to eat; I'd like some baked beans, please.
d He was freezing; the water was very icy.
e Come in, please; explain what has happened.
f Tom loves Indian food; Matthew prefers Chinese food.
g The cake was very pleasant; it tasted delicious.
h The woods were quiet; the only sound was the rustle of the wind in the trees.

2
a The king stood up and said: "I've lost my crown."
b See what's in the box: books, magazines and comics.
c The explorer roared: "Look out!"
d The Prime Minister stood up and said: "Taxes will have to be raised."

e Outside there were farm animals: horses, sheep and cows.
f You will need: pencils, paper and a ruler.
g Dan shouted: "Pass me the ball!"
h Bring these for your ski trip: your passport, a woolly hat and some gloves.

Unit 40: Dictionary work – definitions (page 45)

NB The wording of definitions may vary slightly.

a aisle   a passageway in a church
b isle   land surrounded by water
c berry   a small fruit
d bury   to place something underground
e currant   a dried fruit
f current   the flow in water or electricity
g faint   pale or weak
h feint   pretence
i idle   not doing anything
j idol   something or someone people worship
k key   something that opens a lock
l quay   the side of a harbour
m main   major
n mane   the long hair of an animal such as a lion
o paws   the feet of an animal
p pause   a gap or break in speech
q steel   a manufactured metal
r steal   to take something that doesn't belong to you

Test 1 (pages 46 and 47)

1
a we<u>dge</u>   bu<u>dge</u>   ri<u>dge</u>
b hu<u>tch</u>   sti<u>tch</u>   ca<u>tch</u>

2

verb	present tense	past tense	future tense
draw	I am drawing	I **drew**	I will draw
sleep	I am sleeping	I **slept**	I will sleep

3
a harb**our**   b treas**ure**

4
a thieves   b lorries

5
a slippery   b quiet

6 a nosy b icy

7 a I waited <u>patiently</u> for the bus.
b <u>Reluctantly</u> I walked home when it didn't come.

8 a **k**nife b **g**nome

9 <u>The guard dog slept in the kennel</u> outside.

10 a sister b stairs

Test 2 (pages 48 and 49)

1 a Sam b the birds

2 a **sub**way b **em**bark

3 a Brightly the sun shone.
b Quickly I ran home.

4 a Where are you going?
b Paul and I are going to play cricket.

5 a I went to the library <u>because</u> I wanted a book.
b I kept reading <u>until</u> I was tired.

6 a evident ✓ b signal ✓

7 a The ball was <u>under</u> the table.
b I was pushed <u>against</u> the wall.

8 a art b fed

9 The Eiffel Tower (a metal structure) is in Paris.

10 because become befriend beware

Test 3 (pages 50 and 51)

1 a robbery b contentment

2 a The girl climbed the tree.
b The boy ate the apple.

3 a extravag**ant**
b intellig**ent**

4 The woman (f) sat on the chair (n).

5 a green-fingered
b light-fingered

6 a shi**e**ld b c**ei**ling

7 a (T) b (P)

8 a chargeable b serviceable

9 a The thunder <u>roared</u> and the rain <u>fell</u> heavily. (2)
b The old man <u>sat</u> down tiredly. (1)

10 a deserves another
b than never

Test 4 (pages 52 and 53)

1 <u>They</u> (P) were lost but <u>I</u> (S) had a map.

2 a inspiring b education

3 The ~~naughty~~ monkey ate the banana ~~greedily~~.

4 a I don't know anything.
b He didn't have any money.

5 a I unlocked the box <u>so that</u> I could look inside.
b I watch TV <u>whenever</u> I can.

6 a biography ✓ b asteroid ✓

7 a ar**ound**
b be**hind** or be**yond**

8 a deride b decipher

9 a Don't go away; I want to talk to you.
b The bag contained the following: apples, pears, grapes and bananas.

10 a pane – a sheet of glass
b pain – hurt